3-12-14

PAPER CRAFTS FOR PRESIDENTS' DAY

Randel McGee

Enslow Elementary

an imprint of

Enslow Publishers, Inc.

40 Industrial Road
Box 398
Berkeley Heights, NJ 07922
USA

http://www.enslow.com

*Dedicated to all of our elected officials—national, state, and local,
both men and women—for their service to their fellow citizens
and their work to make our country free and safe.*

This book meets the National Standards for Arts Education.

Enslow Elementary, an imprint of Enslow Publishers, Inc.
Enslow Elementary® is a registered trademark of Enslow Publishers, Inc.

Copyright © 2012 by Randel McGee

Library of Congress Cataloging-in-Publication Data

McGee, Randel.
    Paper crafts for Presidents' Day / Randel McGee.
       p. cm. — (Paper craft fun for holidays)
    Includes bibliographical references and index.
    Summary: "Explains the significance of Presidents' Day and how to make Presidents' Day themed crafts
       out of paper"—Provided by publisher.
    ISBN 978-0-7660-3726-7
    1. President's Day decorations—Juvenile literature. 2. Paper work—Juvenile literature. I. Title.
    TT900.P74M34 2010
    745.54—dc22
                 2010024708

Paperback ISBN: 978-1-59845-333-1

Printed in the United States of America

052011 Lake Book Manufacturing, Inc., Melrose Park, IL

10 9 8 7 6 5 4 3 2 1

Illustration Credits: Crafts prepared by Randel McGee; photography by Enslow Publishers, Inc.; Shutterstock, p. 5. The portraits in the Future President Portrait project were drawn by Emma Jane McGee on October 10, 2010.

Cover Illustration: Crafts prepared by Randel McGee; photography by Enslow Publishers, Inc.

CONTENTS

AUTHOR'S NOTE: Many of the materials used in making these crafts may be found by using recycled paper products. The author uses such recycled items as cereal boxes and similar packaging for light cardboard, manila folders for card stock paper, leftover pieces of wrapping paper, and so forth. This not only reduces the cost of the projects but is also a great way to reuse and recycle paper. Be sure to ask an adult for permission before using any recycled paper products.

The projects in this book were created for this particular holiday. However, I invite readers to be imaginative and find new ways to use the ideas in this book to create different projects of their own. Please feel free to share pictures of your work with me through www.mcgeeproductions.com. Happy Crafting!

Presidents' Day!

When the United States of America won its independence from Great Britain, the people wanted a new form of government to lead their new country. Instead of a king who was born into the royal ruling family like they had under British rule, the citizens of the new country decided to have a president who was elected, or chosen, by the people. A president does not make laws, but he or she has the responsibility to see that laws are carried out and that the government runs effectively. He or she is the commander in chief of the armed forces of the United States and represents the country to foreign governments.

George Washington had been the commanding general of the American army in the Revolutionary War. The American people elected him to be their first president. He was sworn into office on April 30, 1789. He served for eight years. He has been called "the father of our country" due to his lifelong service to the country—fighting for its independence, establishing its government, and leading its people. The new capital city for the United States of America was called Washington in his honor. He was so well liked by the American people that even during his presidency, his birthday, February 22, was celebrated as a holiday in many states.

Many men have served as president since Washington's time. All of them have been men who were dedicated to their country, its laws, and its people. They have come from different backgrounds and have served their countrymen and women in many ways before becoming president. After serving as president, many have returned to their previous careers or continued to serve in other ways.

In 1971, President Richard Nixon issued a declaration making the third Monday in February a national holiday celebrating Washington's birthday. However, it was called Presidents' Day by many states and

businesses who wanted to use the day to honor not only President Washington, but all the presidents who had served their country. In the United States today, Presidents' Day is a day when most national, state, and local government offices and public schools are closed. The crafts in this book can be made before or during Presidents' Day to help you remember the great men who have served our country.

Log Cabin Bank

America has always prided itself as a land of opportunity, where anyone can succeed with hard work and determination. Americans often point to the fact that even a poor person who lived in a roughly made log cabin could become a success. Several men who became president, such as Andrew Jackson, Millard Fillmore, Abraham Lincoln, and James Garfield, started life in log cabins. This log cabin bank can hold coins with pictures of presidents on them. Can you name the presidents on the coins?

What you will need

- tracing paper
- pencil
- light cardboard
- scissors
- construction paper
- ruler
- card stock
- markers, crayons, or colored pencils
- clear tape

WHAT TO DO

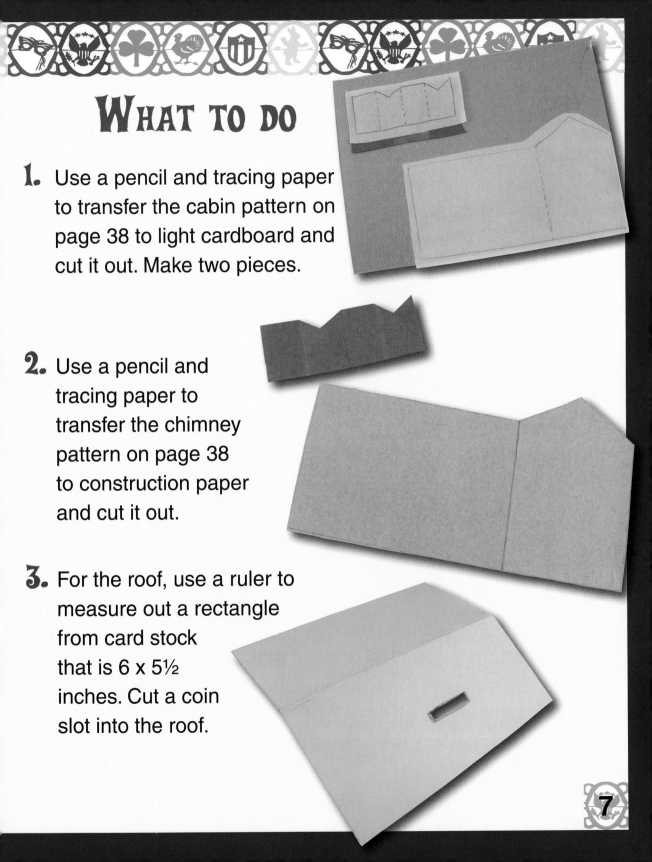

1. Use a pencil and tracing paper to transfer the cabin pattern on page 38 to light cardboard and cut it out. Make two pieces.

2. Use a pencil and tracing paper to transfer the chimney pattern on page 38 to construction paper and cut it out.

3. For the roof, use a ruler to measure out a rectangle from card stock that is 6 x 5½ inches. Cut a coin slot into the roof.

4. Use markers, crayons, or colored pencils to decorate the cabin with log sides, doors, window frames, or other features. Decorate the chimney and roof as you wish.

5. Fold the cabin pattern along the fold lines of the pattern to form the corners of the cabin. Tape the edges of the walls together to form the cabin.

6. Fold the roof piece in half width-wise. Tape the roof to the top of the log cabin.

7. Tape the open side of the chimney closed. Tape the chimney in place on the roof.

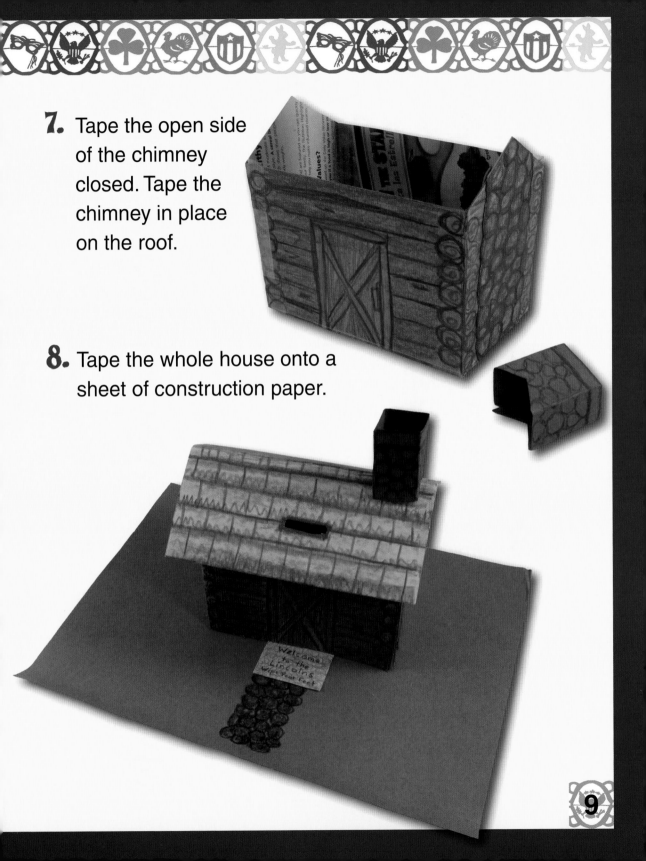

8. Tape the whole house onto a sheet of construction paper.

Washington's Cherry Tree

In 1800, writer Mason L. Weems told the story of how young George Washington had chopped down his father's prized cherry tree with his new hatchet. When the father asked who had cut down the tree, the young boy admitted that he had. The father was proud of his son's honesty. The story became famous; however, Mr. Weems made the story up.

In 1912, Japan donated 3,000 cherry trees to Washington, D.C., to decorate the parks and lawns in the capital. Each year the city celebrates the beautiful blossoming of these trees.

What You Will Need

- tracing paper
- pencil
- construction paper—brown and green
- white glue
- light cardboard
- pink tissue paper
- scissors
- clear tape

WHAT TO DO

1. Use a pencil and tracing paper to transfer the tree trunk pattern to a piece of brown construction paper and the base pattern to green construction paper. See page 41 for the patterns.

2. Glue the brown trunk pattern to one side of a sheet of light cardboard. Glue brown construction paper to the other side of the cardboard. Let dry. Do the same with the green base pattern.

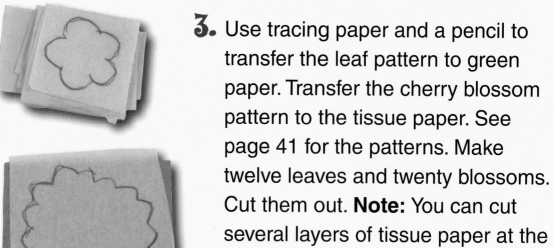

3. Use tracing paper and a pencil to transfer the leaf pattern to green paper. Transfer the cherry blossom pattern to the tissue paper. See page 41 for the patterns. Make twelve leaves and twenty blossoms. Cut them out. **Note:** You can cut several layers of tissue paper at the same time to make many copies.

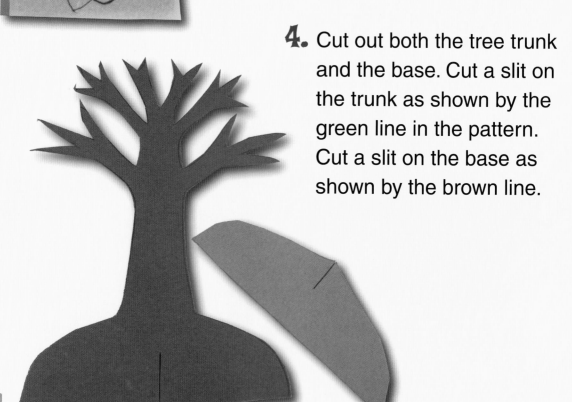

4. Cut out both the tree trunk and the base. Cut a slit on the trunk as shown by the green line in the pattern. Cut a slit on the base as shown by the brown line.

5. Glue the leaves to the branches of the tree. If you wish, glue some green paper grass to the brown base. Let dry.

6. Put a drop of glue in the middle of each blossom and place them on the leaves. Let dry.

7. Put the trunk and base together by slipping the slit at the bottom of the trunk into the slit at the top of the base.

8. Put clear tape along the line where the trunk and base meet.

PRESIDENT'S BUST—EGG AND PAPER SCULPTURE

The United States has had many presidents since George Washington took office in 1789. A bust is a sculpture that features the head, neck, and shoulders of a person. This project will help you create a bust of an American president. Who will you choose?

Note: You can find portraits of all of the presidents at http://www.whitehouse.gov/about/presidents/

WHAT YOU WILL NEED

- a hollowed or plastic egg
- tracing paper
- pencil
- card stock
- scissors

- white glue
- old newspapers (to line work area)
- acrylic paints
- paintbrush
- permanent markers

- cotton balls, batting, or craft hair (optional)
- clear tape
- construction paper

WHAT TO DO

1. Use a hollowed real egg or plastic egg for your project. **Note:** Have an adult help you if you hollow a real egg. Use a large sewing needle to poke a small hole in the small end of the egg. Poke a larger hole, about the size of a pea, in the large end of the egg. Have an adult blow against the small hole until the egg white and yolk are forced out the larger hole in the bottom. Save the egg white and yolk in a bowl for use in cooking. Rinse the hollow egg with water and let it dry on a paper towel.

2. Use the tracing paper and pencil to transfer the ear and nose patterns from page 40 to the card stock and cut them out.

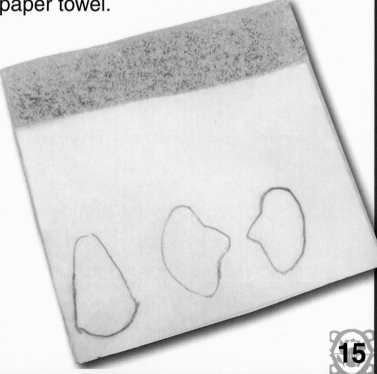

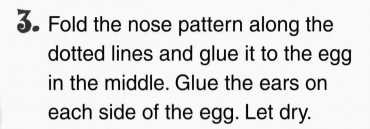

3. Fold the nose pattern along the dotted lines and glue it to the egg in the middle. Glue the ears on each side of the egg. Let dry.

4. Use acrylic paints and a brush to color the egg as you wish. Let dry. **Note:** Working on old newspapers will keep paint and ink from staining the work area.

5. Use permanent marker to add eyes, mouth, and other features to the face.

6. Use the cotton balls, batting, or craft hair to add wigs or hair to the head as you wish. You may want to color the cotton with marking pens before you glue it on. Be sure to let it dry thoroughly.

7. Copy the shirt and tie patterns from page 40 to card stock. Cut them out. Tape the edges of the collar together. Decorate the tie.

8. Glue the head to the collar. Let dry. Tape the bust to a piece of construction paper.

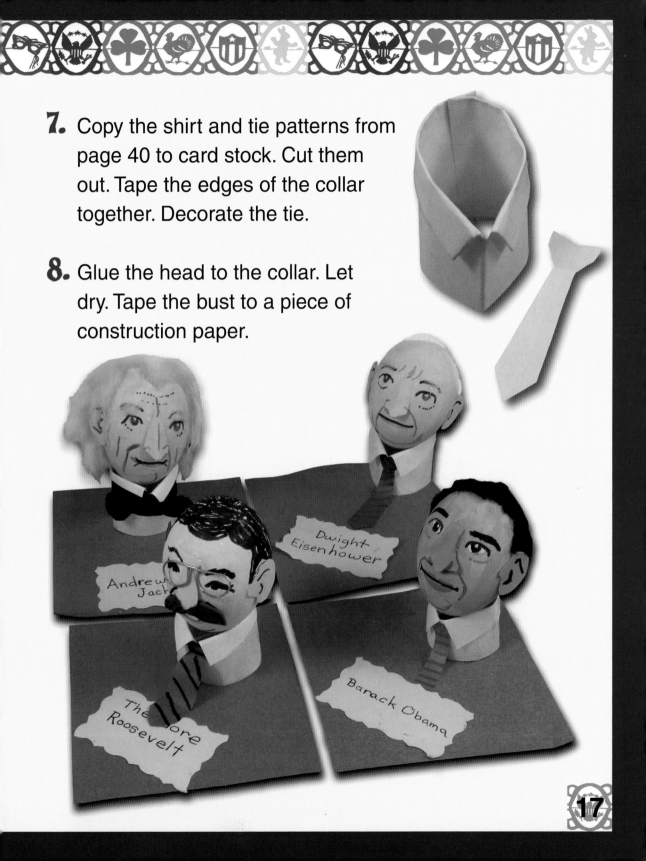

Dwight Eisenhower

Andrew Jackson

Theodore Roosevelt

Barack Obama

THE WHITE HOUSE POP-UP CARD

President John Adams, the second president, and his wife, Abigail, were the first to move into the building that has been called the President's Palace, the President's House, and the Executive Mansion.

WHAT YOU WILL NEED

- ✎ tracing paper and pencil
- ✎ white card stock
- ✎ crayons, markers, or colored pencils
- ✎ scissors
- ✎ white glue
- ✎ construction paper

It is a white building with a large portico, or porch held up by four columns. It has been the home and office of each president since John Adams. Theodore Roosevelt officially gave it the name the White House in 1901. It has become a symbol for the position of the president and for the leadership of the United States.

18

WHAT TO DO

1. Use tracing paper and pencil to copy the patterns from page 43 to white card stock.

2. Color the card and pieces with crayons, markers, or colored pencils as you wish.

3. Cut out the patterns along the solid black lines.

4. Fold along the dotted lines on the main building pattern. Gently push the building design forward as you fold the card closed. Open it again.

5. Fold the roof piece along the dotted line. Glue the roof piece in the center of the top of the building. Let dry.

6. Fold the portico piece on the dotted lines. Glue the top of the portico to the roof flap. Put a drop of glue at the bottom flap of the portico piece and glue it to the base. Let dry.

7. Fold a 9 x 12-inch piece of construction paper in half, like a book, and glue it to the back of the White House card.

8. You may want to add a small American flag to the top of the portico.

FLAGS OF THE UNITED STATES

The first official American flag had thirteen stars on a blue field with thirteen stripes of red and white, representing the original thirteen colonies. The number of stripes changed over the years until it was decided to keep the thirteen original stripes and add stars for every new state. This project shows some of the different flags that have flown over the White House and the years in which they were used.

WHAT YOU WILL NEED

- tracing paper
- pencil
- light cardboard
- white card stock
- crayons or markers
- star stickers (optional)
- scissors
- hole punch
- yarn or string

22

WHAT TO DO

1. Use tracing paper and a pencil to transfer the ring pattern from page 39 to light cardboard.

2. Transfer the flag patterns from page 39 to white card stock.

3. Color the flags and decorate the ring as you wish. On the back of each flag, write its name, date of use, or other interesting facts.

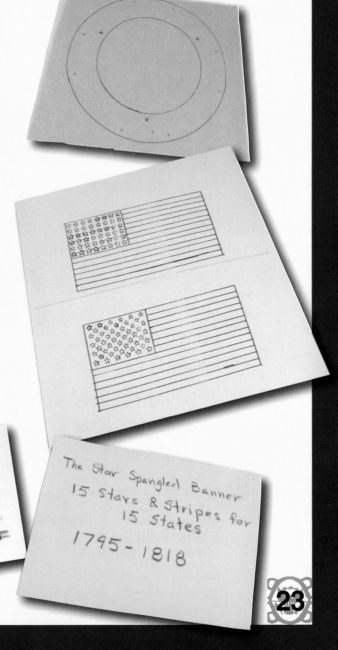

The Star Spangled Banner
15 Stars & Stripes for
15 States
1795 - 1818

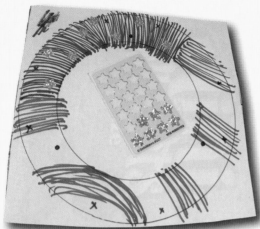

4. Cut out the patterns from the light cardboard and card stock.

5. Use a hole punch to make holes on the ring indicated by the Os.

6. Cut three 16-inch pieces of yarn or string. Tie them to the ring through the holes.

7. Use the hole punch to make holes in the ring and flags in the places indicated by the Xs.

8. Use different lengths of yarn or string, 10 to 14 inches long, to tie the flags to the ring through the remaining holes.

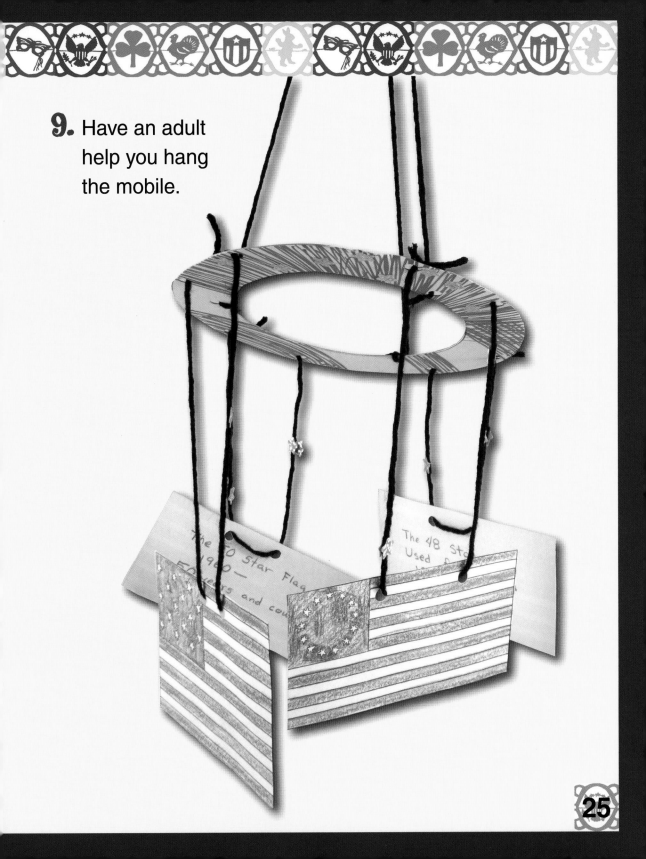

9. Have an adult help you hang the mobile.

A Three-cornered Hat and Collar

It was the fashion during the first years of the new American republic for well-dressed men to wear a hat with three corners, a high collar, and a tie called a jabot (zhah-BOH). Many paintings of our early presidents show them wearing these items of clothing. This project will help you make your own costume so that you will look like an early American president.

What you will need

- ✎ tracing paper
- ✎ pencil
- ✎ black poster board
- ✎ white butcher paper
- ✎ scissors
- ✎ clear tape

WHAT TO DO

1. Use tracing paper and a pencil to copy the hat pattern from page 42 to the black poster board and the jabot patterns from page 42 to the white butcher paper.

2. Cut a strip of white butcher paper 2 inches wide and long enough to fit loosely around your neck. You will need the strip to be at least 13 inches long.

3. Cut the pattern pieces from the white butcher paper.

4. Tape the jabot pieces together at the straight end with the largest one on the bottom, the medium piece in the middle, and the small one on top. Curl the bottom edges of the pieces slightly with your fingers if you wish.

5. Tape the jabot pieces to the middle of the white paper strip.

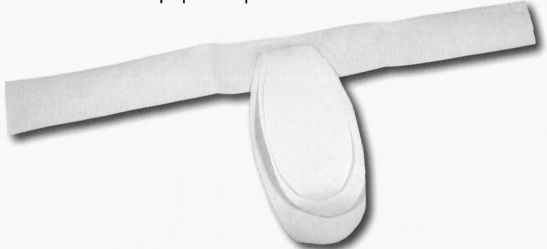

6. Have an adult help you gently wrap the paper strip around your neck and tape it together so that it fits comfortably and loosely.

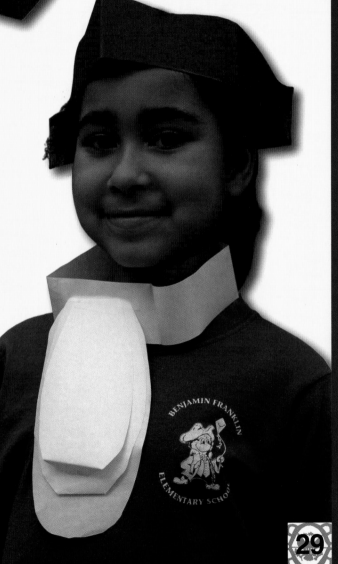

7. Cut out three hat-pattern pieces from the black poster board.

8. Tape the short edges of the pattern pieces together to form a triangle. Gently place the triangle on your head. To make a good fit, pinch a corner or two, and tape the corners together until the hat fits snugly and comfortably.

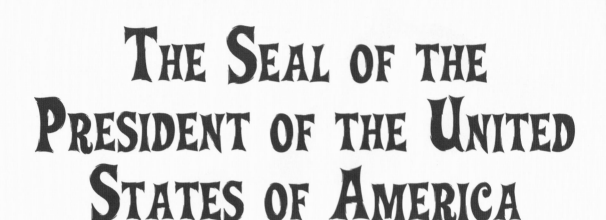

The Seal of the President of the United States of America

The president of the United States has an official seal that represents his or her office and authority. The eagle in the center holds an olive branch, symbolizing peace, in one claw and arrows, symbolizing power, in the other claw. The eagle holds in its beak a banner that says *E PLURIBUS UNUM,* Latin meaning "From the Many— One." The eagle is surrounded by fifty stars for the many states that form one country.

What you will need

- pencil
- computer paper
- white glue
- light cardboard
- crayons, markers, or colored pencils
- scissors

WHAT TO DO

1. Use a pencil to copy the patterns from page 42 to the computer paper.

2. Glue the computer paper to light cardboard.

3. Use crayons, markers, or colored pencils to color the pieces as you wish.

4. Cut out the pattern pieces.

5. Glue the eagle in the center of the circle. Glue the shield on the eagle. Let dry.

6. Use the seal as a decoration where you wish.

FUTURE PRESIDENT PORTRAIT

The Constitution says anyone who is born in the United States or born to parents who are citizens, is at least thirty-five years old, and has lived in the country for at least fourteen years is eligible to run for president. You may be president someday!

WHAT YOU WILL NEED

- tracing paper
- pencil
- light cardboard
- poster paint
- paintbrush
- scissors
- white glue
- crayons or markers
- clear tape
- a 5 x 7-inch drawing or photograph of yourself (Ask permission from an adult when using a photo.)

WHAT TO DO

1. Use the tracing paper and pencil to transfer the patterns from page 40 to light cardboard.

2. Paint the pattern pieces on one side with the poster paint and brush. Let dry.

3. Cut out the pattern pieces.

4. Glue pieces onto the frame as you wish. Let dry.

5. Decorate the frame with crayons or markers as you wish.

FUTURE PRESIDENT

6. Tape a drawing or photograph of yourself to the back of the frame. Make sure it is facing the right way.

7. Have an adult help you hang the framed picture where you wish.

PATTERNS

The percentages included on the patterns tell you how much to enlarge or shrink the image using a copier. Most copiers and printers have an adjustable size/percentage feature to change the size of an image when you print it. After you print the patterns to their true sizes, cut them out or use tracing paper to copy them. Ask an adult to help you trace and cut the shapes.

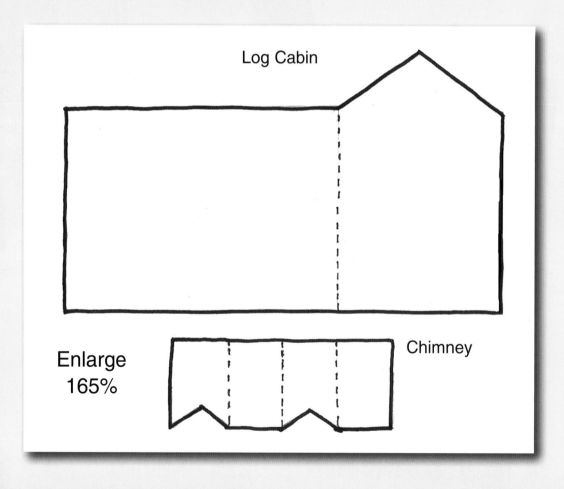

Log Cabin

Enlarge
165%

Chimney

Flag Mobile Ring

Enlarge 250%

50-star Flag

48-star Flag

Star-spangled Banner Flag
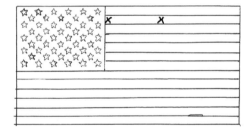

Betsy Ross Flag, 1776

Enlarge 150%

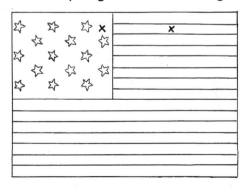

Presidential Bust Shirt Collar

Tie

Ears

Nose

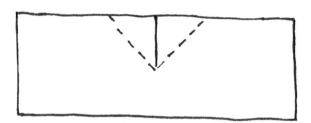

Enlarge 175%

Future President Frame

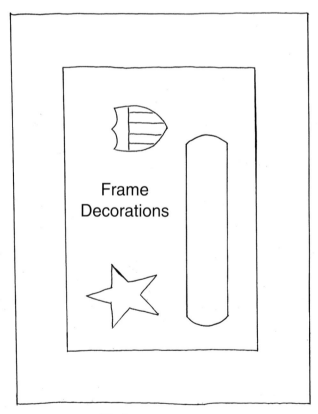

Frame
Decorations

Enlarge 225%

Cherry Tree and Base

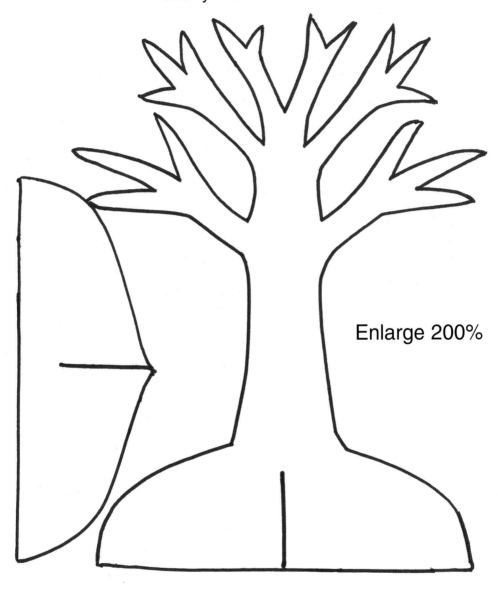

Enlarge 200%

Cherry Tree Leaf

 Cherry Blossom

Jabot Patterns

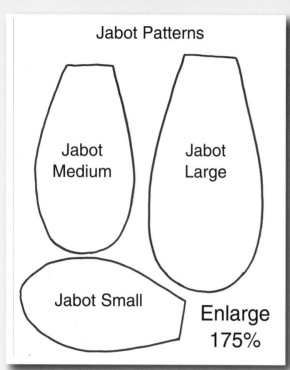

Jabot
Medium

Jabot
Large

Jabot Small

Enlarge
175%

Three-cornered Hat Pattern

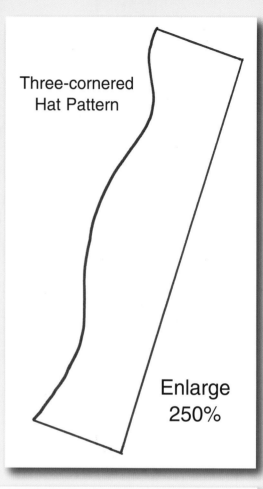

Enlarge
250%

Presidential Seal Base

Enlarge 250%

Presidential Seal Eagle (layer 2)

Enlarge
250%

Presidential Seal Shield (layer 3)

White House Pop-up

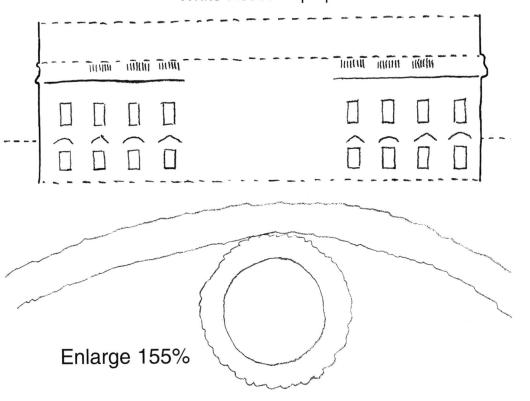

Enlarge 155%

White House Portico and Roof

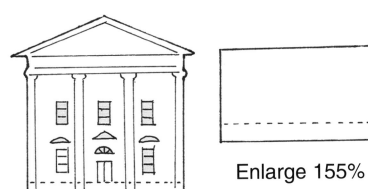

Enlarge 155%

READ ABOUT

Books

Peppas, Lynn. *Presidents' Day*. New York: Crabtree Publishing Company, 2010.

Trueit, Trudi Strain. *Presidents' Day*. Mankato, Minn.: Child's World, 2008.

Internet Addresses

DLTK's: Presidents' Day Activities

<http://www.dltk-kids.com/crafts/presidents.html>

Kaboose: Presidents' Day 2011

<http://holidays.kaboose.com/presidents-day/
  presidents-day.html>

Kids Craft Zone: Presidents' Day Crafts

<http://kidscraftzone.com/category/
  Presidents-Day-Crafts.aspx>

Visit Randel McGee's Web site at
<http://www.mcgeeproductions.com>

INDEX

ABOUT THE AUTHOR

Randel McGee has been playing with paper and scissors for as long as he can remember. As soon as he was able to get a library card, he would go to the library and find the books that showed paper crafts, check them out,

take them home, and try almost every craft in the book. He still checks out books on paper crafts at the library, but he also buys books to add to his own library and researches paper-craft sites on the Internet.

McGee says, "I begin by making copies of simple crafts or designs I see in books. Once I get the idea of how something is made, I begin to make changes to make the designs more personal. After a lot of trial and error, I find ways to do something new and different that is all my own. That's when the fun begins!"

McGee has also liked singing and acting from a young age. He graduated from college with a degree in children's theater and specialized in puppetry. After college, he taught himself ventriloquism and started performing at libraries and schools with a friendly dragon puppet named Groark. "Randel McGee and Groark" have toured throughout the

United States and Asia, sharing their fun shows with young and old alike. Groark is the star of two award-winning video series for elementary school students on character education: *Getting Along With Groark* and *The Six Pillars of Character*.

In the 1990s, McGee combined his love of making things with paper with his love of telling stories. He tells stories while making pictures cut from paper to illustrate the tales he tells. The famous author Hans

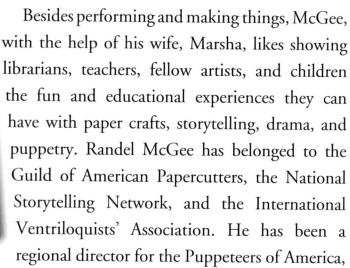

Christian Andersen also made cut-paper pictures when he told stories. McGee portrays Andersen in storytelling performances around the world.

Besides performing and making things, McGee, with the help of his wife, Marsha, likes showing librarians, teachers, fellow artists, and children the fun and educational experiences they can have with paper crafts, storytelling, drama, and puppetry. Randel McGee has belonged to the Guild of American Papercutters, the National Storytelling Network, and the International Ventriloquists' Association. He has been a regional director for the Puppeteers of America, Inc., and past president of UNIMA-USA, an international puppetry organization. He has been active in working with children and scouts in his community and church for many years. He and his wife live in California. They are the parents of five grown children who are all talented artists and performers.